"Gunner" James Moir.

This book is published strictly for historical purposes.
The Naval and Military Press Ltd
expressly bears no responsibility or liability of any type,
to any first, second or third party, for any harm,
injury or loss whatsoever.

THE COMPLETE BOXER

BY

"GUNNER" JAMES MOIR
EX-HEAVY-WEIGHT CHAMPION OF GREAT BRITAIN

The Naval & Military Press Ltd

Published by

The Naval & Military Press Ltd
Unit 5 Riverside, Brambleside
Bellbrook Industrial Estate
Uckfield, East Sussex
TN22 1QQ England

Tel: +44 (0)1825 749494

www.naval-military-press.com
www.nmarchive.com

*In reprinting in facsimile from the original, any imperfections are inevitably reproduced
and the quality may fall short of modern type and cartographic standards.*

CONTENTS

CHAPTER		PAGE
I.	THE BOXING REVIVAL	9
II.	A BOXER'S EARLY TRAINING	14
III.	THE BOXER'S EDUCATION	27
IV.	TRAINING	35
V.	SPARRING PRACTICE	55
VI.	RING-CRAFT	61
VII.	THE PRACTICAL VALUE OF BOXING AS A MEANS OF DEFENCE AGAINST AN ATTACK BY HOOLIGANS	74

LIST OF ILLUSTRATIONS

	PAGE
"Gunner" James Moir . Frontispiece.	
The Classical Pose	15
Blocking a Left Head Lead	23
Ducking a Left Head Lead with Counter	29
Left Upper-cut to Chin	33
Double Counter to Right Head Lead	37
Arm Exercise: First Position	41
,, Second Position	43
Side Stepping a Left Body Lead with Left ready for Upper-cut	47
Effect of a Right Cross to the Jaw	49
Side Stepping and Countering a Left Head Lead	51
Right Head Lead Side Stepped and Countered with Hook to Jaw	53
Knocking Down a Left Body Lead and Right Counter to Head	59
Side Step to Left Body Lead	63
Right Hammer Blow to Head	67
"Knocking Out" a Beaten Man	69
A Cross Buttock Throw	71
A Back Heel	73
A Block to the Back Heel	75
The Knee Upper-cut	77

CHAPTER I.

The Boxing Revival.

WHAT a change has taken place during the years which have elapsed since the last edition of this treatise was published. Then, boxing had sunk to possibly the lowest place it has ever held in public estimation in this country, while to-day it is probably the most popular of all sports, as indeed it should be, seeing that it is the national one.

But how can the average boxer be expected to maintain, to say nothing of improving, his form, if he is only afforded such meagre opportunity for practice? Sparring practice and exhibition work are frequently supposed to keep one in trim, but as a matter of fact, unless the boxer is particularly careful they are distinct deterrents to progress. I would even go so far as to say that a boxer who is compelled to depend mainly on exhibition boxing for his livelihood is simply bound to go back. He can't help doing so. For among other things, he must, in order to give a good exhibition, play down to the level of his sparring partner (almost inevitably a less skilled man than himself), he has to " play light," and this will naturally exert a serious effect on his punch, he gets careless through having to lay himself open to punishment for display purposes, and, worst and most serious of all, he is liable to indulge in a good time, put on flesh, and generally get out of condition.

There is only one really satisfactory way in which a boxer can assure himself of a steady improvement, and that is by engaging in serious contests pretty frequently, say, five or six times a year. Now, owing to the number of light-, feather-, and bantam-weights there are about, a fair proportion of our lighter divisions have been afforded opportunities for something approaching this number of contests, but somehow or other, heavy- and middle-weight contests do not materialise in anything like the same proportion.

Worse than this, even, is the method adopted by one or two boxing promoters who run a fairly regular series of contests. For these they engage a staff of boxers, paying them a regular but by no means generous salary, and pitting them against each other, or rather shuffling them together in such order as they fancy will best attract their regular patrons.

This system may appear all right on paper, but in practice matters arrange themselves in such a way as to lead one to entertain a pretty strong suspicion that these contests are decided more or less to order, that is to say, that they are really little else than exhibitions, though labelled serious. The boxers themselves dare not complain, and if told to lose—well, they lose as quickly and easily as they can. They are usually advertised as fighting for a purse, and may even at times—when receipts have been extra good, and the promoters attacked with a fit of generosity—receive some small bonus. But as a matter of fact, they are simply boxing for their wages. Defeat or victory will have little effect on their future either way. The man in the street may be gulled into thinking more or less of them, but the men who matter know too much. These last will even underestimate the boxer's skill. They will know him to be just a member of a troupe, with no greater prospect of championship honours than that possessed by the minor wrestlers belonging to one of the great Continental championship wrestling tournaments, which were held periodically in various towns, the contestants just moving round in a body as employees of the particular champion who accepts the engagement, and pays the wages.

Champions can never be made under this system A boxer may be as clever as could be wished with his fists, foot and head work, but unless he develops his thinking capacity, his ring-craft, he will never be much good. He wants to be able to out-manœuvre his opponents, to divine their moves, and to be able to counter and defeat them, and he will never be able to do this unless he has a powerful incentive. It must be worth his while, for his boxing career will at best be but a comparatively short one, during which he is anxious to save all he can for his later years. And how is he to do this out of a few pounds a week?

If he is a steady, brainy fellow, he must necessarily anticipate the future by looking out for an occupation for his spare time, one at which he can become sufficiently proficient to step into when his boxing career is finished, with the result that his interest is divided.

The National Sporting Club cannot possibly provide contests for all the boxers in the country, or for anything approaching the number. What is really wanted is a multiplication of such institutions. But they must be real clubs. Not merely boxing arenas, so-called clubs, with or without genuine membership, but run almost solely for the pecuniary benefit of the manager, who arranges the fights—and also the results, in accordance with the way the betting goes.

As every reader must be aware, many professional boxing contests, outside the National, are open to suspicion. The honesty of the National fights are guaranteed by the reputation of the members. All that they desire to see is the victory of the best man, and should any pair of boxers agree to " fake " a fight there, they know full well that they will be discovered, and that thenceforth, no matter what fame they may subsequently achieve, they will find the Club closed to them.

Now, there are plenty of sportsmen as honest as the National members scattered up and down the country. Surely it should be by no means impossible for them to come together and found clubs of a similar high standing in most of the big towns throughout the country.

The interest and success which has attended the formation of " promoters' clubs " here and there attords ample proof that such clubs would be successful. All that is lacking just now is a sufficient experience of boxing and boxers', or rather promoters', methods, to enable the members to detect trickery, fakes and arrangement. This will soon be gathered, but, unfortunately, when it is, the result is usually to disgust the decent man and to make him retire altogether from participation in the game, instead of making him resolve to stick to it and purify it.

The decline of English boxing may be laid almost solely at the door of the sportsmen, the real sportsmen of England. They expected honesty and straight dealing from rogues, and when they were disappointed, as was natural, were too lazy to step in and provide it for themselves. The present generation is now offered an excellent opportunity for improving on their fathers' and grandfathers' methods, but unless they can summon up sufficient energy, it is to be feared that we shall see another decline and possibly a complete extinction of our National Sport.

CHAPTER II.

A Boxer's Early Training.

WHERE is one to find promising boxing material ? Well, everywhere or anywhere. One never knows. True, that most of the heavy- and middle-weight material of recent years has been discovered in the ranks of the Army and Navy, but this has, as a rule, been disappointing.

So much so indeed, that I have heard many good critics declare that nothing great was ever to be expected from a soldier or sailor.

" Oh! he's a soldier, a slow, clumsy fellow, he'll never be any good." This is a remark one often hears, and, unfortunately, one that is frequently justified by events. I served my full time in the Army, and won several heavy-weight championships in India, South Africa, the Mauritius, and elsewhere, but found that I had plenty both to learn and to unlearn when I entered the professional ranks. In fact, I sometimes think that unless I had possessed a naturally heavy punch of my own I should never have made much headway.

In the Army, for instance, we usually get to business as quickly as we can, and keep at it hammer and tongs until we have finished. Few of us ever cultivate the art of saving ourselves and allowing the other man to exhaust himself. So that when we run up against a really smart professional, who understands ring-craft, we sail right in, hitting right

The Classical Pose.

and left, without being particularly careful as to where our blows are going to land.

Our old opponents in the Army or Regimental Championships were just as anxious to get their blows in as we were, and so were generally well within range, with the result that the man who hit quickest, hardest, and most frequently was pretty certain to secure the verdict. Besides which, it was all over in three rounds and neither of us had much time to spare.

Up against the professionals, the soldier instinctively follows the same method. He forgets that the fights are, as a rule, going to last much longer, so he swings and drives away, with the other fellow just slipping out of the way, blocking his blows and waiting his chances. A round or two passes, and the soldier finds that while he has scored once or twice perhaps, his opponent has been careful to save himself, and that he himself has wasted most of his strength on the air.

He is badly in need of a breather, but the moment he commences to take it, the experienced man gets to work, puts in a well-directed blow, which shakes him up, and soon has him in difficulties. The soldier's only idea of saving himself is to swing wildly, and so steady his opponent, for all his experience has taught him that the latter (if he follows the example of the men he used to fight) will be rushing in to finish him, and will therefore be certain to receive it.

But, unfortunately, he won't be. He will either avoid it altogether and finish his man as he tries to recover his balance, or else he will close in to him, pounding away at his body with both hands. In either case it will be, as a rule, all U.P with the soldier. The spectators shake their heads, and say, "Ah, what did I tell you?"

They take no further interest in the soldier, and he, after one or two spasmodic efforts, concluding that there is no opening for him in the boxing profession, retires, and the ring thereby probably loses a really good man, who only needed a few lessons in ring-craft to qualify for first-class honours.

Some of you may, perhaps, have been present at the National when I fought Tommy Burns, and in that case will doubtless recall the preceding contest between Jack Scales and Corporal Sunshine.

The Corporal had it all his own way for the first three rounds, so much so indeed, that I doubt if an offer of 1,000 to 1 on him would have found any takers at the end of the third round. Scales could just stand up and no more. But the Corporal had taken too much out of himself, was in a desperate hurry to finish matters, swung wildly two or three times, and missed altogether, overbalancing finally, and stumbling into Jack, who was able to pull himself together and deliver a short-arm jab on the mark, from which the Corporal never recovered. He just staggered about, swung and missed for another round and a half, serving as a punch-ball for Scales, who was gradually coming round, until he (Sunshine) finally rolled out of the ring altogether, beaten really by himself.

Now, a boxer who means to prosper profits more by his defeats than by his victories. That is to say, if he doesn't get defeated so often as to lose heart altogether. I have seen many a loser who, if taken in hand by a really smart and intelligent instructor, would have proved a most profitable investment.

I wonder, by the way, why the modern boxing instructor so rarely does this. In the old days, men like Mendoza, Gentleman Jackson, Nat Langham, and others, who, retiring from the ring, opened boxing academies, were always on the look-out for promising talent, which they would carefully nurse until they felt pretty confident that they could back their pupils against a man of fair reputation.

They would then find backers among their wealthier patrons, and launch their man on his career, of course participating in his early winnings, thereby earning both advertisement and profit for themselves.

It wasn't a bad policy, and might be pursued today, but, unfortunately, the majority of modern instructors possess neither the necessary initiative, intelligent anticipation, nor even the ability to bring their protégés out successfully.

They adhere too closely to the old, stereotyped methods, founded on the style best adapted to London Prize Ring rules, and cramp a novice's style in such a way as to render him a fairly easy prey to the looser-limbed and more speedy—and brainy— American, or English boxer adopting American methods. For alas,! it must be confessed, that the modern style of boxing owes more to American innovation than it does to British. Take the ordinary position to commence with.

The classical pose for a boxer, or rather the one which is usually impressed upon the British novice, is to stand left foot foremost, toes pointing to the front, feet from 15 to 18 inches apart, with the heel of the right foot about three inches to the side of the line of the front foot, and at right angles thereto, legs slightly bent, forward shoulder raised a trifle to protect the chin, the weight balance rather on the right foot, or, at all events, more than on the front one.

The novice is further instructed to keep his left arm well out towards his opponent, slightly bending it at the elbow, and in a line with the left nipple. The right arm to lie across the chest with the elbow well into the side, the back of the hand uppermost, the fingers of the clenched hand resting on the left breast, and the inner side of the forearm aslant across the body, so as to guard the " mark," or point where the ribs divide. Various other points, such as the careful preservation of this posture, both in advance or retreat, are insisted upon, from the standpoint that it is better for a man to lose a bout, provided that he box in orthodox fashion, than that he should win it by the practice of methods which depart from the classic style.

There is much to be said for these rules and regulations, perhaps. They certainly tend to steady a man, to enable him to watch points, to cover himself well, and yet be at the same time in good posture for attack, but, on the other hand, it has the effect of turning out those, who are trained by it, all made after a certain pattern. They all box in the same style, hit, stop, and get away, or try to do each and all of these things in perfect imitation of each other, with the verdict going to the man who, by virtue of a shade of extra quickness, a slightly longer reach, or possibly harder punch, can manage to get home either first or most effectively.

One could wish for nothing better, if the pupils of this school were never called upon to meet any opponents other than their fellow pupils, but once they run up against an unorthodox fighter, the whole beautiful scheme falls to pieces. The finished British article, finished, that is, according to the good old classical method, has only been led to expect, and therefore CAN only anticipate ONE style of either attack or defence on the part of any opponent.

Any other style or system he has been taught is a bad style, both unpleasing to look at and demonstrably ineffective in THEORY. Unfortunately, however, for the classically trained boxer, he discovers it to be lamentably successful in practice—at his expense. He finds himself all at sea when opposed by an unorthodox boxer, a man who comes in crouching, totally ignoring the axiom that a boxer should take full advantage of his height, while if the man advances now with his right hand to the front, at another time with his left, who will even come up with both hands advanced, turning full to the front, he knows not what to make of it, nor what attack to make preparation for.

The Most Useful Style.

In actual practice I doubt if it matters much how a man poses himself when actually fighting. True, that most of the leading boxers take up a position fairly close to the classical, approved style when posing before the camera, but watch them in an actual match, and you will find that they pay little heed to attitude or position. The easiest and loosest is the best, and the more it is varied the better, for the simple reason that by continually threatening to come in and lead with either hand, your opponent is uncertain as to what he is to expect, and the more confused you can make him, the easier prey will he become.

Tommy Burns, for instance, would spar up with the right or left foot advanced, but usually the left, when the right would be from 12 to 20 inches to the right rear. He would stand almost square to his opponent, and hold his hands, now shoulder high, now sometimes only just above waist level, or again, with one fully extended to the front, to keep his man well away from him (but this last was rare).

There is one big advantage in standing square to your man, which the supporters of the old style overlook, for from that posture a right-hand lead at either the head or the body can be delivered both more easily and more effectively.

You can test this for yourself by sparring up to an imaginary opponent. Stand up in the old approved style, as described above, and try a right-hand head lead. You will find, if you watch yourself in a mirror while delivering it, that it is almost impossible to bring it into play without completely disclosing your intention to any quick and ready witted antagonist. First, the right arm has to be shifted from its position of guard across the chest, and in doing this, the right shoulder must almost inevitably be pulled back. Two clear indications these, which the other man has ample time to prepare for while you are stepping forward and bringing your arm across. Indeed, the only method of bringing off a successful right head lead from such a position is to feint successfully with your left first, and this is by no means a certain draw, while in any case you are exposing your own face and body to a pretty severe counter from the other man's left, which will only have about a third of the distance to cover that your right will have.

The chance of a successful right body lead is similarly lessened for the same reasons. It can be guarded against with either or both arms, and can also be easily and heavily countered with a straight left.

But try either of the same blows when standing square on. Your right hand will be but little behind your left and has but slight extra distance to cover. It is close enough even to feint with, and feinting with both hands is more useful than feinting with only one. You are in a position to either stand away and hit, or jump close in for " in-fighting,"* whichever you please; and are in no way hampering any subsequent attempt to bring the left into play immediately after, should you so desire.

You are, of course, offering a larger target for assault, but then, if you have cultivated smart footwork, you can easily and quickly withdraw this from danger. And here again lies another advantage of the full-faced position, that your freedom of movement is much less cramped. You find that you can both advance and retire much more quickly, that is, of course, always supposing that you have steadily

---

* For fuller hints see "**Infighting**," by FRANK KLAUS (Middle-Weight Champion of the World), 2/-, post free 2/3. 'Boxing' Office, Thanet House, 231, Strand, W.C.2

Blocking Left Head Lead, Countering Left to Body.

practised the art of always being on your toes. Naturally, it is given to few heavy-weights to be as quick on their feet as Tommy Burns was, but it is a quality which can be cultivated if a man starts practising it early Heavy-weights will certainly have to do so in the future, if they aspire to championship honours. It is going to be the most valuable quality a boxer can possess. Hitting power has been cultivated to such an extent that stopping and guarding all blows are practically impossible; the arms won't stand the strain, so that a man must necessarily slip away from them. He must be in and out in a serious long drawn-out contest or he will be down and out long before it has run its full measure of rounds, while in a three-round amateur affair he will, if he stays in and leads, be probably checked by well-timed counters, until these have tired him sufficiently for the man who has been on the defensive for the first two minutes or so to outpoint him completely with rapid hitting in the last 40 seconds or thereabouts.

Hitting.

Much praise has been lavished on the good old style of hitting straight from the shoulder, but one sees little of it nowadays between two well-matched first-class men. They know better than to waste time in drawing back for the purpose, and realise further that by so doing they will disclose their intentions. The boxer of the future must learn to hit short, that is to say, he must practise hitting from an already advanced arm, either by merely straightening it, or, when possible, by swinging his body in and hitting a bent-arm blow, travelling say from eight to fourteen inches, and gathering its force from the shoulder and forearm muscles.

I have now, I think, enumerated the principal points which should, in my opinion, first occupy a boxing instructor's attention. He should coach his pupils in the full art of the full-faced position, paying his particular attention to their footwork, training them to keep always on their toes, moving quickly forwards and back, with the feet turning slightly outward ready to slip either to right or left, as the case may warrant. The exact motion, whether of advance, retreat, or sideways, should be, as a rule, very slight, just enough to spoil an opponent's distance judging, and never enough to carry the man out of actual distance himself. He may wish to go right away or even right past his man at times, but this he can acquire later. What he needs to commence with is simple freedom of movement and of action.

Then, as to the position of his hands and body. Here the boxer's peculiarities must themselves be consulted. It is often said that I don't crouch low enough myself, and, in fact, that I rarely crouch at all. This may possibly be one of my faults, but that is because the crouch has never seemed comfortable to me, and a boxer should, above all else, feel comfortable. So let him stand up or stoop as seems best to him, provided that his freedom of movement is in no way interfered with.

As to his hands, well, if he crouches, one of these will probably be head-high, with the other either at shoulder or waist level, but both should be, I think, best advanced slightly. One fully extended will serve the purpose of keeping one's opponent at a distance, but will, in that event, have its hitting power somewhat diminished. The knees are best bent slightly, and the weight of the body supported equally on both feet, which will assist rapidity of movement.

All these things can be learnt by practice at shadow fighting, that is, by sparring with an imaginary opponent, in imitation and under the supervision of the instructor. Actual sparring practice, stamina and punching exercises can come later, and may be dealt with in the next chapter.

CHAPTER III.

The Boxer's Education.

As a rule, the first things which the novice is set to learn consist entirely of the various leads, guards, and counters, and for that reason a large proportion of the first edition of this book was occupied by a lengthy description of these.

Space which I fear was mainly wasted, for after all a mere catalogue should suffice. The leads themselves are important, for the simple reason that in amateur and other short contests, where two men are fairly equally matched, the decision is awarded to the one who has done most leading, that is to say, that the majority of points accrue to the man who initiates most attacks.

A lead, whether with the left or right at the head or body, or as a double lead, which last is really a spring in to close quarters, with two simultaneous or quick following blows from each hand, must be a blow sent right home, and not merely a feint, or threatened blow. Their mere enumeration will fully describe them, with the remark that from a man who usually stands in the classic attitude the left head lead may be most usually anticipated. It is such an easy blow to strike for a man standing in the stereotyped position, since he has only to advance, or straighten his arm, stepping in at once, and the blow has gone, while provided he does it quickly, making performance jump smartly with intent, there is no need for any preliminary feint. True, that the lead despite the ease and readiness with which it can be delivered, may be just as readily guarded, slipped or countered, and that the counter to same, either by means of a simple left cross-counter, or in combination with any parry, is likely to be pretty severe, yet the temptation to let go such an easy blow is too great to be resisted.

For one thing, the boxer adopting the classic style will ordinarily be normally working his left arm in and out like a piston, and so can deliver the lead by the simple process of adding a little force to his ordinary forward sway. It may get home and it may not, and, if smartly executed and followed, or rather accompanied by a quick side-step, may reasonably be expected not to necessarily invite severe retaliation, even if unsuccessful. That is unless your antagonist be quick footed, stands square to you, and is a good two-handed fighter, when he can push smartly with his right, checking your arm about midway, and at the same time countering heavily on your body with his left.

For he then has the advantage of the INNER position, and can throw or push aside your attacking arms. It is immaterial whether he attacks your body or your face, but he will probably go for the body, since when leading at the head with the left, a man frequently raises his right or guarding arm to protect his own face.

It is a good plan, by the way, in guarding all blows, and particularly in guarding leads, to anticipate these, as far as possible, by checking the arm, rather than by stopping the blow. The striking arm

Ducking Left Head Lead, Countering Short Right Jab to Body, Left Held Ready for Right Follow to Left Head Lead.

can be checked by pushing the striking shoulder or biceps, either of which methods will not only arrest the blow itself, but will permit of the checking fist being slid along into a blow itself.

While on the subject of leads, guards, etc., a few words will amply suffice to dispose of the average kind of blows of this description, as delivered by the upstanding side-turning boxer. Take, for instance, a good old-fashioned right head lead. The man delivering it may or may not feint first; he should, properly speaking, have not only done something of the kind, and previous even to that, should have got well home on your body or head, and thereby demoralised you a bit, before he attempts such a risky blow; for, in every case, unless you are really badly demoralised, you can, as a rule, " see " this blow coming.

In fact, you can usually anticipate all right leads from a classic-style boxer, because he invariably, or almost invariably, pulls his right shoulder back or at all events raises his arm from its usual position and draws it in to gather force. You guess that it is coming, and can rest fairly confident that it won't be a pleasant one when it does come. Nevertheless, you have, as a rule, a fair amount of time for all that you have to do. You can stop it easily and smartly by just pushing your own left straight into his face as he swings forward.

This will be quite effective enough as a rule, for he will be coming forward and will meet your jab halfway. Then his blow will have to come right round, while yours goes straight, and the straightest road is always the shortest, while if you are standing full on to him, or nearly full on, you can play up to almost any kind of lead far more effectively.

Advantages of the Full-faced Position.

These can be grasped most readily by a man who takes the trouble to gain a full idea of what " reach " really means.

A long reach is notoriously a very valuable asset to a boxer, but even this will be deprived of most of its usefulness if its owner has never troubled to really study distance judging, which consists of so aiming your blow that it arrives at its object with its full force at the precise spot that object will occupy when your blow arrives. Reach, after all, is only an accessory to hitting, and is only valuable when you want your blow to travel a considerable distance.

You may not, and indeed probably will not, pull out anything like your full reach in hitting the vast majority of your blows, simply because these will be delivered at pretty close quarters, and will therefore only need to travel over a short distance. They will be aimed at head or body, and, unless you have a marvellous insight into your opponent's brain, will probably be directed at the position occupied by either at the moment of starting.

That is why side-stepping, ducking, etc., come in so useful, but both of these ruses have slight drawbacks of their own. A duck or swift move of the head, for instance, is liable to disturb one's balance slightly, while a side-step may (although it should not do so, if possible) interfere with your chances of replying to the lead which you have side-stepped.

Now, when standing full on, you present a well-defined target, which your opponent can scarcely avoid hitting at. So that by merely turning sideways, right or left, you can, by extending the arm left in play, easily counter his lead, while you will at the same time have withdrawn your own head and body into safety. You will have outreached him in fact, no matter how long his reach may be, for he will almost certainly have sent in a shortish-armed blow, and will thus be out of distance.

Hitting short, out of distance that is, is always a most exasperating thing to a man. It takes a lot out of him for one thing; and for another it is liable to jar his arm pretty badly, if he does it frequently, for, as you know possibly, or can easily discover if you don't, it hurts far more to hit the air forcibly when you expected to hit a more solid object, than if you come into hard contact with the object itself. So cultivate this full-faced position, and carefully practise the side turn out of reach, going now to the left and now to the right. You can bring your right leg back just as well to a left-hand lead as you can to a right one, and, by carefully practising both methods, can bring either into action as may be most convenient for you.

As will have been noticed, I am not proposing to make a text-book of this edition, to run through a mere catalogue of the ordinary leads, counters, etc., and the usual school methods of delivering them or dealing with them. I did this in the first edition, and can refer my readers to that more or less valuable effort, or to any other boxing text book, should they desire the information contained therein. But

Quick Step to Close Quarters with Left Upper-cut to Chin after Feinting a Body Lead.

as they will, in any event, have to attend some school or other should they desire to study boxing, they will be certain to gather there all the practical information which they can desire on the subject.

Personally, I am now inclined to fancy that none of it is particularly necessary. A boxer wants to hit his opponent as hard, as often, and as cleanly as he can, and it will not advantage him much to know the correct designation of the blow he has got in, so long as he HAS got it in. He will, I think, be able to profit more by a few practical hints as to the easiest methods of letting blows go to advantage, and of avoiding them or minimising their effect, if by chance they may be directed at himself.

So that the items of first importance, after balance, steadiness and quick movement have been studied, are surely those of hard-hitting, and the capacity to stand punishment.

These belong properly to the boxer's early education, but as they are qualities in which he can never be said to have perfected, they may be properly dealt with in another chapter.

CHAPTER IV.

Training.

THIS is naturally one of the most important departments of any form of athletics, but is frequently regarded by boxers, as indeed by most athletes, as being only of occasional importance.

A man goes into training for a match, a race, or a contest of any description, and during the period allotted for the purpose he very possibly does train and train hard, but between whiles seems to think that he need not necessarily take any particular care of himself.

A very bad policy this, for the hard or well-trained man who allows himself to go out of condition will usually be found to do so pretty badly. Not infrequently he puts on flesh, gets slack and lazy, and on going into training again finds that he has not only a lot of flesh to get off, but that the training itself is very irksome and disagreeable.

He doesn't enjoy it, and therefore fails to derive anything like full benefit from it. Every time he does this, he finds his training to be a harder job. He grows to be less and less inclined for the work, goes stale frequently and easily, and, in fact, becomes incapable of ever again getting into the pink of condition.

Now, it is often believed that a boxer's day is usually done soon after he has passed his thirtieth year, but I am disposed to hope that I may preserve my form somewhat longer than this. It won't be my fault if I don't. I am close on forty now, and yet I certainly feel both fitter and younger than I did a few years back. But then I have never allowed myself to get out of condition.

I kept myself in a constant state of half-training, if I may so describe it, and consequently I did not have a particularly hard job when I started to get ready for another big fight.

To a certain extent, I will admit this to be obligatory in my case. For, with a distinct tendency to make flesh, it would not have been policy for me to allow matters to slide.

Then again, a man may pride himself on his punch, but unless he exercises care, this is always liable to deteriorate in power. The punching muscles need to be kept in good trim, both in driving power and in speed, while if one practises assiduously one can always discover fresh wrinkles for making various blows more effective, and these little discoveries are the most valuable a boxer can make.

For cultivating and developing hitting power, there is, after all, nothing to compare with the punch-ball. Every other appliance, and there are numerous ones, can be dispensed with, but the punch-ball can neither be dispensed with nor improved upon.

Ball Punching.

I have been responsible for a booklet on this subject,* and need not, therefore, expand on it here, but there are one or two points which should, I think, receive attention.

First and foremost, I would advise all boxers, when indulging in ball practice, to avoid all fancy

---

*Ball Punching. By "Gunner" Moir. Price 9d. net, by post 10d. "Boxing" Offices, Thanet House, 231, Strand, W.C.2.

Double Counter to Right Head Lead, the Lead being Half Blocked with Left, which is then sent on Temple, and Right to Chin.

work like poison. Certainly both forehead, back and side head play are worth attention, seeing that they are good neck exercises, and a boxer needs a strong neck if he needs anything, but elbow play and pretty work generally are mere waste of time. The boxer punches a ball partly as a means of flesh reducing, wind and eye-developing exercise, but chiefly as a punch cultivator. He should, therefore, go in for it with the latter end in view, and the other objects will achieve themselves.

Hit the ball as hard as you can, and hit it true. Get to work as fast as you can. Even at tattoo, don't just let the ball hit your fists, as so many do, save, of course, by way of an occasional necessary breather, but make most of your short half-arm blows as hard as you can make them. Don't be content merely to put in all your hard hitting practice solely in the shape of swings or long drives. You will have to pull back for these, and if you can only hit with your full force by pulling your shoulder back, you will find yourself sadly handicapped in an actual ring contest, for the mere fact of doing so will immediately advise your adversary of your intention.

Indeed, in case I forget to state it later on, there are practically only two occasions when the shoulder can be safely pulled back. Firstly, when it is back already from a side-step, a side turn, or a retreat, and the arm can therefore be swung without any premonitory indication; and, secondly, when your opponent is reeling and you want to send in a tremendous blow, just to finish him off, for he will not then be likely to take note of much.

The blows you really want to make as hard as possible are the short ones, the jabs and digs at close quarters, sent in either with bent arm, or by merely straightening a bent one. Then two can come as a postman's knock, if you carefully practise it. It is well worth practising, for it will be found most effective. A drive in the ribs may be repeated once and occasionally even twice before your opponent has time to cover the spot, and if both or all three of these be really forcible, they will go far towards finishing the contest altogether.

But remember that neither the second nor third can be pulled back more than three or four inches at the outside if they are to be repeated, and unless considerable time be devoted to practising them they will be absolutely harmless. The best method is to get close up to the ball, drive it back as hard as you can, and meet it sharp and hard, that is, HIT it, don't allow it only to hit you as it rebounds. It sounds easy, doesn't it? but if you have done any ball punching you will know how difficult it is to really hit it in time. Yet it is nevertheless the best, if not the only way of practising.

I usually make a practice of fighting three or four rounds with my punch-ball, allotting the full three minutes to each round and taking my minute rest in between by walking up and down with a towel over my shoulders. This, by the way, is a point of some importance. At every daily practice, no matter how this be prolonged, nor of what it consists, whether you spar, box with your own shadow, punch the ball, skip, or go in for other exercises, NEVER SIT DOWN TO REST. Keep moving all the time. Don't allow yourself to get cool, or your muscles to get stiff. Drape a towel over your shoulders to guard against chills, and walk up and down your gymnasium. Keep moving, whatever you do.

Then, again, it isn't a bad plan to vary your punch-balls a bit. Use light, well-inflated balls for fast work, and heavier ones for developing the hitting muscles. For the latter purpose again, the use of a light, say, a pair of 1 lb. dumb-bells, is by no means a bad idea. These should be grasped firmly in each hand, so as to add force to your blows. And bearing the force of these blows in mind, don't forget either to wear soft bandages or fingerless gloves under your ball-punching ones when you are at work. For you must remember that you are going to hit every bit as hard as you will hit in an actual contest, and that you will also be hitting much more frequently. You will, therefore, be running the risk of knocking your knuckles up unless you safeguard them, a risk it is advisable to avoid as much as possible.

Finally, don't be satisfied with just standing up to your ball and hammering away at it. Slip it, dodge past it, and jump round it. You may as well make use of it for slipping practice as well. It will assist you in your footwork, will teach you to turn quickly and, above all, to hit at and get home on a slippery, dodging antagonist.

Even if you should mis-hit the ball pretty frequently as you dodge round it, and, of course, you often will at first, this won't matter much. The ball will only come back at you in awkward, unexpected fashion, and thus afford good practice in dodging,

Arm Exercise: First Position.

meeting, and steadying awkward attacks when you yourself are in difficulties. It needs a steady eye, coolness, and calm nerves to straighten a ball again when it has been mis-hit or grazed, and is swinging out of the true, and each of these three is an asset which it is well worth your while to acquire.

Shoulder, Arm, and Chest Development.

Some of the American critics described my rope-climbing exercises as fool " training," but then they have also told their readers that I was a sailor, and published a lot more misinformation about me.

I just pull myself once or twice up a longish rope with my hands only, and am still satisfied that by so doing I considerably strengthen both my shoulders and hitting muscles. It isn't bad forearm exercise either, while, in addition, it helps to deepen the chest, which, as I think you will agree, is a distinct advantage. Naturally, I don't overdo it, nor do I make it a regular daily item of my training.

One exercise I certainly do go in for pretty assiduously, and that is perhaps best described by illustration. I rest the palm of one hand on the floor and, supporting myself on that and the sides of my feet, alternately push myself up to the full extent of my arm and lower my body again until it is within an inch or so of the floor. The exercise is shown well in the two accompanying photographs, and should be repeated up to twelve times daily with each arm. It is a bit laborious, perhaps, but it is very strengthening, not only to the arms, but to practically every muscle in the body, including the abdominals.

Arm Exercise: Second Position.

Abdominal Exercises.

These last call for very particular attention. For not only does every man need to keep them in good working order, for digestive purposes, but a boxer should develop them very particularly, as a protective measure. He is liable to receive pretty heavy punishment over his stomach and lower ribs, and if he can cover these parts with strong muscles, he will be better able to face it with a fair amount of equanimity.

He should, therefore, devote at least a quarter of an hour, if not more, daily to these muscles, for which I can personally recommend at least four different exercises.

The first consists of lying full length on your back on the floor, and holding in each hand a light, say, a 5 lb. dumb-bell close to your head. Then rise into a sitting posture, and sink back gradually. You will at first find it easier to dispense with the weights altogether, as the rising and sinking will be quite difficult enough in themselves. But add the weights as soon as you can, and gradually increase, say, from 1 lb. up to 5 lb. Repeat twelve times.

Then reverse the performance by raising your legs to right angles with your body, subsequently attaching a gradually increased weight to your ankles, and raising your legs with the additional strain. Repeat this also twelve times, keeping the legs perfectly straight.

Another abdominal exercise, which will strengthen the arms, shoulders, and legs into the bargain, consists of bending over until you are supporting yourself on your hands and feet. Then alternately bring your legs quickly up as far under your body as you can. Spring smartly each time, of course, bending your knees each time you bring them forward. Repeat twelve times with each leg alternately.

The fourth exercise is merely stooping down and trying to touch the floor with your finger-tips, or, if possible, the palms of your hands, keeping the legs perfectly straight the while. Repeat this, say, twenty times.

Skipping.

This is certainly one of the most valuable of all forms of exercise. Personally, when training hard, I skip for about twenty minutes daily, say, from 2,000 to 2,500 skips without a break. It is a splendid method of making you quick on your feet, strengthening your leg muscles, loosening your joints, and developing your wind. Don't shirk the skipping rope by any means: skip steadily and increase your pace as fast as you can. Fast skipping is the thing, variations are only useful as a form of rest. Don't hesitate to let the rope out a bit, and to skip slowly if you find yourself getting tired and flurried, but go back to fast work again as soon as you steady down. Speed is a great thing, and can be cultivated, but stamina or staying power is even better, and you will find few things so valuable in cultivating this as the fast and steady use of the skipping rope.

Walking.

Personally, I walk a great deal. Some people even say that I overdo this department. But then there are few things I enjoy so much, and a day has rarely passed during these last two or three years when I have not put in my ten or even twenty miles on the road. This might possibly be too long a stretch for many boxers, and possibly six, or at most seven miles, would be all-sufficient for the average man, even during a period of strict training. In either event, he should cultivate a good, fast action, with occasional trots and sprints. He should always, where possible, run up a hill at a smart pace, as he will find this far and away the finest breathing or lung exercise in existence. For this reason, he should, wherever possible, get out into the country for his walks, although, when making Shepherd's Bush my training quarters, I used to walk daily from my home in Lambeth, through St. James's and Hyde Parks to the Bush, then in the afternoon to Kew or further afield still, and put in another ten miles or so at a fast walk or trot.

Even on tour I never neglect my daily walk, and, despite the late hours necessitated by my music-hall work, rise pretty early and do my seven or eight miles (sometimes more) every morning.

Keeping in Condition, and Strict Training.

The points dealt with above have been treated more or less as belonging to the strict preparation for a serious contest, but should on no account be neglected during ordinary seasons. A boxer should make a practice of covering at least five miles every day all the year round, at as smart a walking pace as circumstances will allow. He should also make a practice of putting in a bit of ball punching, say

Side Stepping and Pushing Down a Left Body Lead with Left in Position for Upper-cut.

at least twice a week, even in off seasons, while a brief daily spell (say, five minutes or so) with the skipping rope would not hurt him. The abdominal exercises should certainly be practised at least once a week, and the climbing-rope (if this be patronised) quite as often if only to keep one's hand in, but one climb only will suffice. Sparring practice between whiles will naturally depend on opportunity, but whenever possible, one should try to secure, say, one bout weekly, or perhaps fortnightly, during the summer in order to keep in trim. Light work, even if indulged in daily, will not necessarily make a man stale, and although this said light work is apt to play the mischief with your punching powers, this can be remedied by hard and fast punch-ball practice.

For strict training, that is to say, when preparing yourself for a serious fight, you must follow a regular routine. Rise at seven, say, and breakfast, then get out on the road, and do your walking exercise, long or short, according to your observation of results. Don't fancy that because I believe in long-distance walking this will necessarily suit your requirements. If training for the first time, you might try how a six-mile tramp, trot and sprint will suit you, and if you find that you enjoy it thoroughly, and seem to prosper on it, with an appetite for more, well, then, lengthen it out a bit.

When you get back, have a good brisk rub down, a shower bath, a thorough massage, and a short rest before dinner. After which you can laze about a bit till, say, three or four o'clock, and get to your gymnasium work. Go into this with a will. Skipping, ball punching, shadow fighting (as earnestly

Effect of a Severe Right Cross to Angle of the Jaw.

and smartly as though you were really engaged with a serious opponent), abdominal and arm exercises, as described above, and sparring practice.

For this last get as many partners as you can, and, above all, get men who won't mind being knocked about. The more and the harder they retaliate the better for you. Don't be particular about the length of the rounds, and if you should happen to knock one of your partners out by accident get another man to take his place without delay. Remember that in your actual coming contest you may not improbably have to face a man who presses you hard just when you are badly distressed, and that you will in consequence need plenty of practice in the arts of "stall-him off," and of saving yourself under such circumstances. So don't hesitate to take on a fresh opponent, when you would prefer to lie down and die. Don't overdo it, by the way, and get yourself knocked about so badly that you have to give up training altogether for a day or two; but should the men be able to give you more than you bargained for, remember that you are having a real good coaching.

If things are going fairly smoothly, and you find that none of your partners are capable of extending you overmuch, you can devote a portion of your rest-time to extra ball practice. A minute or so of hard and fast ball work, between the rounds, particularly if you are at all short of sparring partners, will freshen you up well, and will assist in developing your stamina. Don't on any account sit down to rest, but if you must take a breather, walk about briskly while you are having it.

Side Stepping Left Lead to Head, at same time Pushing Opponent's Arm to Force Exposure of Ribs to Severe Right Counter.

Rubbing Down and Massage.

Whatever you do, be sure and engage a good trainer or attendant. One, above all, who thoroughly understands the way to rub you down and massage you, for this is of the first importance. You will have put in some pretty stiff exercise, and will have naturally strained your muscles and encouraged them to become hard and stiff, and this is the last thing you wish to happen. Your muscles must be kneaded thoroughly, pulled, pinched and slapped, and brought into soft, pliable and supple condition. This in an art in itself, and can only be acquired by practical experience. Get a man like Harry Andrews,* or my brother Charles, if you can find one, and place yourself in his hands.

The Boxer's Diet.

A good many boxers, like other athletes, have fads in this department, but personally, I don't think that a man need trouble or worry much about the matter He can consult his own tastes, eat and drink anything he cares for, provided it be good, plain, wholesome food, and ordinary roast or boiled meat, toast or stale bread, with a fair quantity of green vegetables and fruit. Potatoes and pastry should, of course, be carefully avoided. Three good meals a day should suffice, the third coming about seven o'clock, although a plate of soup or a very light meal might be allowed, perhaps, at, say, 9.30, but this is not always advisable. Bed not much later than

---

* **Massage and Training.** By HARRY ANDREWS. 1/6 net, by post, 1/9. "Boxing" Offices, Thanet House, 231, Strand, London, W.C. 2.

Right Head Lead Side Stepped with Right Hook to Chin.

10 p.m., as at least eight to nine hours' sleep is absolutely necessary. An occasional cigarette won't hurt, but tobacco should never be indulged in to any extent. As regards drink, well, spirits, of course, should be altogether taboo, but a glass of beer now and then, say, two or three, won't hurt anyone. A little tea or coffee, a cup or so of Bovril, with perhaps a glass of hot milk before retiring, will provide all the liquid nourishment required.

Going Stale.

This calamity, which must always be guarded against during training, may be best recognised by the flow of perspiration. If this shows signs of diminishing considerably and suddenly in quantity, you may be certain that you are threatened with staleness, while if it be accompanied by a sluggish feeling and disinclination for work, you are probably in for a bad attack. A strong tonic will often exert a beneficial effect, but the best remedy is to knock off all work for a day or two. Just go for a short, brisk morning walk, do a little shadow fighting, and lounge about for the rest of the day, reading or talking. Go to a theatre, if you like, and avoid worry, and you will soon find that you have pulled yourself round again. But don't hesitate to knock off at once.

CHAPTER V.

Sparring Practice.

As previously hinted, the best way of learning boxing is to spar and indulge in bouts with as many and as varied opponents as you can. Each and every one of them can teach you something, however little knowledge they may possess themselves. An absolute novice, a raw rough diamond who hits and swings wildly, without aim or idea, is often every bit as awkward a customer to face as even a polished champion. For one reason alone, that you will never be able to anticipate what he is going to do next, and you may catch a nasty swing on the jaw when, by every rule, he should have been clinching to avoid punishment.

In a previous chapter I stated that exhibition boxing was, on the whole, distinctly harmful to the ambitious boxer. Well, it is as a rule, or rather a certain kind of it is. Suppose a man, for instance, to be compelled to depend for a fair portion of his livelihood on his engagements at amateur club displays. He will there be pitted against leading members who are anxious to put up a good show against him, and whom (with a view to future engagements) he must assist in that, more or less, laudable endeavour.

There is a tacit understanding on these occasions that the professional must on no account inflict any serious damage on his amateur antagonist, and that while exhibiting tremendous vigour and force in his deliveries, he shall exert an equal amount of care to avoid making these at all violent in reality. Despite all this, I have myself come across amateur boxers who, even during previous rehearsals and with positively vicious intent in public, strained every nerve to put me out. They would come rushing in, swinging wildly with both hands, and sparing neither pains nor effort to achieve the distinction of having " knocked out " the champion of England.

These were not pleasant experiences, and as, despite all warnings, they would persist in their attempts, I was compelled to hit out hard in self-defence to escape the threatened indignity. Of course the cases referred to were extreme ones, but I have alluded to them personally in order to show the awkwardness of having to restrain one's natural and instinctive methods, at the risk of receiving punishment, just because it doesn't do to hit out in an exhibition bout, and to support my argument that an overdose of this sort of exhibition work tends to cramp one's style.

But there is exhibition boxing and exhibition boxing. I have had a pretty full experience of one variety on my various tours. Up and down the country I have met with numerous opponents, many of them rather unpolished, but quite a respectable number of whom had had a pretty fair experience. And they weren't all exhibition spars either, save in name. I was willing enough to make them exhibition displays, but I was quickly advised that my opponents meant serious business. They went to work with an evident eye to serious business, and had to be treated seriously.

Naturally, I felt a bit sorry for them, and would rather, far rather, have adhered to my programme; but these gentlemen enjoyed a local reputation, and had come to the hall accompanied by a fair number of their friends and admirers, all anxious to see them maintain or possibly glorify it.

I got some good slipping and avoiding practice, but more than once got some good give-and-take practise as well—well, perhaps more give than take, but that was only because I had to choose between them, and preferred the former.

They came up in every conceivable variety of style. Edgeways and full-faced, full of the most serious intentions, and usually backed by grim determination. But, as a rule, they weren't particularly quick, and I discovered a rather smart way of stopping them speedily. I coaxed them in pretty close, and then, just as they would pull back for a right drive, say, would tap them up under the chin. It looks and sounds easy, and would not probably come off against a good many, but there are times when it might, particularly if you feinted for a body blow and came up smartly. The blow is a species of upper-cut, and can be applied suddenly when drawing back from a clinch or a little spell of in-fighting. Break away suddenly by stepping back with your right foot and then jab the left up smartly, holding the right ready to guard.

Which reminds one that there is too much long-range work indulged in, as a rule, in sparring practice. This is a mistake, since in actual contests most of the business is done at close quarters. Try double leading more, and jump in, for if you fail to land you can always clinch, and nearly every man is in sad need of good in-fighting practice.

If he closes in well after having ducked, say, a left head lead, he should find his opponent's right side practically exposed to attack, as the other man's hand should be away somewhere well over his left shoulder, so that he can pound away merrily for quite a time at his adversary's ribs. And rib punishment tells, particularly if it be frequently repeated round about the same spot. Every breath taken subsequently by the man so visited will cause him considerable inconvenience, not to say pain, and once a man's breathing powers are interfered with, he is—well, by no means so formidable an opponent.

Every boxer who understands his business prefers the body as a point of attack, to the face or head. A good cross-counter, hook, or swing to the jaw, may finish the contest quicker, but then it is by no means so certain of getting there. A slight duck or move of the head, and the effort is wasted. So very many blows which are or have been aimed at the jaw, with the laudable intention of securing a knock-out, only succeed in landing on the back of the head, because the shoulder has been raised and the head ducked forward. This hurts the knuckles, and does the recipient little or no harm. No real opportunity of getting well in to the jaw should, of course, ever be neglected, but don't get trying for it every other second. It's a waste of time and effort, and leaves you badly open to reprisals, while if the other man only keeps his head, covers his chin up well by rais-

Knocking Down Left Lead at Body and Countering with Right to the Head.

ing his shoulder, and ducks skilfully, you won't really have many chances of bringing off a knock-out. The right cross-counter is, of course, the favourite knock-out blow, but then, if it fails to get there, well, the man who has employed it may find himself knocked out instead. The safest plan is to attend to the body first. There is a large target to aim at, and if plenty of practice at in-fighting has been indulged in, it should be frequently scored upon. Get there often, and confine your attentions to the face, at first, to such opportunities for upper-cutting, short jabs and hooks, as may present themselves. These will worry your opponent, while your body work will distress him, and you will, by-and-by, be able to concentrate more of your attention on knock-outs.

CHAPTER VI.

Ring-Craft.

FIRST and foremost, never underrate your opponent; secondly, and of almost equal importance, don't overrate him. He may have earned a terrible reputation for a certain punch, of which you have received ample warning, but don't allow this to occupy the whole of your attention, as otherwise your thoughts will be so occupied in looking out for it that you will altogether miss any other pet useful punches he may possess, until your attention is unpleasantly drawn to them.

Above all, remember that, properly speaking, there is only one man present in whom you are at all interested—your antagonist—and don't allow yourself to be distracted by anyone else.

I speak feelingly on this subject, as I fell into this error with Tommy Burns. There were several contributory causes, which need not be dealt with here. Some were, perhaps, intentional, and, if so, were only evidence of the fact that Tommy put his plans into execution on occasion some hours before he entered the ring, and certainly some minutes before the call of "Time." Others were domestic, sickness at home, and so forth, and yet another was the perhaps natural anxiety of my seconds, both official and self-appointed.

These last were far too numerous, and certainly far too obtrusive. How they contrived to muster in such force I have never been able to discover, but once there it was absolutely impossible to restrain their exuberance.

Anyway, the combined circumstances worried me to such an extent, that I actually allowed my attention to wander on three or four occasions from Tommy himself to Mr. Corri. We had clinched, and Burns had trapped my arm in such a way as to give the referee the idea, from where he was sitting, that it was I who was holding. He consequently warned me on several occasions, and I permitted myself, foolishly, to become sufficiently exasperated to draw Mr. Corri's attention to the actual state of affairs, with the result that I had my face cut open in two places. This happened very early on, and was a serious handicap, as Tommy made a point of keeping these wounds open.

I have not related this experience with any idea of explaining my defeat, but rather as an example of very sharp but perfectly legal tactics, of which I was, unfortunately, the sufferer. I might add that the trick was never repeated after Mr. Corri had entered the ring, and was therefore in a position to see everything that went on.

By the way, I might quote another little move of Tommy's that came off very successfully on that occasion. As you are possibly aware, I rely rather extensively on my body hitting, particularly at the lower ribs. Burns had naturally studied this point, and took very particular precautions against it. He clinched a good deal, or we both did, whichever you prefer, but whenever we did so, Tommy came in well covered up, hands up in front of his face, head well down, under my chin, which, by the way, he butted once or twice (accidentally, I believe), and elbows well out to the front. And nearly every time

Side Stepping Left Lead with Left Ready to send to Ribs.

I went for those ribs he pushed my arms down with his elbows, coming up smartly for my face immediately afterwards with the fist belonging to the arm which he had just put to such useful purpose.

This pushing down business with hand, arm, or elbow is a pretty useful move to employ against a body hitter. You have the upper position, and can hardly miss. True, that you run a risk of exposing yourself to an unintentional foul blow by driving the fist below your belt, but a slight side-slip will avoid most of this danger, and anyway you will have seriously disturbed his balance, and can upper-cut him or get a good chance at his jaw, free from all risk of retaliation.

It is a good thing, indeed an indispensable one, to size your man well up in the first round, provided he gives you time, and doesn't start rushing you straight away. But even if he does this, you will have learnt all you want to know by that time, and can go to work pretty confidently. You will have an anxious moment or so perhaps, but if you keep cool and steady, you can meet his onslaught with a straight drive. This will, if well administered, pull him up short, and if it doesn't send him down, will perhaps even better serve your purpose by affording you an opportunity to jump in on him and shake him to pieces by a series of short, fierce half-arm jabs and hooks. You will have to be quick about it, or he will drop before he has received all that you would like him to get. But whether he goes down first or subsequently, be ready for his rising.

He may regain his feet in a demoralised condition, when, of course, if you get at him quickly, you can reduce him practically to pulp, but if he is a real game charger, like Tiger Smith or Bill Squires, well, he needs careful watching. For while he has been down (and remember that when sent to the boards you can and should take at least eight or nine seconds before you rise again, unless you have first risen on one knee, when you can take $9\frac{1}{2}$ seconds), he will have had ample time to fully survey the situation and his future chances. These he realises to be a bit discounted, and may very possibly in consequence make up his mind to try another rush. Bill Squires did when he fought Burns the first time, and according to Tommy's own version he very nearly pulled it off. Anyway, he caught the ex-Champion one right in the mouth, and, as the latter admits, staggered him badly, with the sole resource of clinging on to the Australian in order to keep himself from falling.

Similarly, I had to send the Tiger down three or four times before he gave up the rushing game. I waited on him each time, and quite possibly had I adopted other tactics and rushed at him as soon as he rose, he might have caught me unexpectedly.

With the opposite style, against the man who hangs back and fights cautiously, you must adopt very different tactics. You don't want to expose either yourself or your hand right at the beginning by opening the business too quickly, so must lure him out of his caution as soon as you can. You can do this best by presenting an opening, keeping well on the watch to spring back into safety if he shows signs of taking quick and big advantage of it. Still, there are various ways of going to work, and one

E

which may be practised with advantage is to raise your arms, thereby exposing your body, ready to knock his blow down if he accepts the bait.

But don't go in too close in doing this, and should you risk it, mind that you are quick with that downward push.

A variation may be introduced, by exposing your face, with the hands held low down, but in that event you must duck quickly and get to close quarters smartly, with a special eye open for upper-cuts, as you go in.

Unless you fancy yourself specially at all or any of these moves, the safest plan, perhaps, is just to go in well covered up, with head bent well down, one hand raised to its level and elbows bent, ready to meet blows at the face or upper chest, the other hand held about waist high, and well back, ready to drive into his ribs as soon as you get to comparatively close quarters.

While against any opponent whom you respect. it is always advisable to change your tactics as much as possible. Try and keep him wondering as to what you are likely to do next. Keep him on the move, and if possible force him to do most of the aggressive work. Get in and clinch as soon as he looks dangerous, and whenever you can do so with comparative safety. Visit his ribs, if possible, as you come into contact, and then take a rest against him. Let him do the pushing away, and be careful as you break. If he doesn't absolutely push you off (when you can, of course, punch him with impunity before he has recovered from the exertion) it is, as a rule, advisable to jump clear, unless you are

Right Hammer Blow to Head with Left Ready to Guard Right Body Counter.

parted by the referee, or have so pasted him on the body that you can risk a blow at him as you break.

Make a point of taking the centre of the ring, and of keeping it whenever possible. By so doing, you force your opponent on to the outer circle, can usually keep him moving, and have so arranged matters that he has to cover more ground than you have to do. This advantage is not so very difficult to secure, if you cross each other before recommencing each round, and can turn sharp round the moment you reach the centre, when he must rush if he is to dispossess you. There are, of course, exceptions to this rule, and one important one is when you are trying to make a man lose his temper, by presenting him with seeming chances, while you keep just out of his reach.

When doing this, it doesn't matter particularly where you are as long as you avoid being rushed into a corner or on to the ropes, but should you foresee that this last is inevitable, spring back early, and at such distance as may tempt your adversary to rush you there, side-stepping smartly as he comes, a manœuvre which, if smartly executed, will possibly lure him into trouble and momentary helpless entanglement, of which you may take advantage, with the additional score of assisting him to lose his temper and self-control.

Should you be absolutely forced on to the ropes, don't neglect to secure a possible push off from them, which will help you in a jump into clinch, which is practically your only method of escaping a very bad time, if you are unable to side-step and slip away.

"Knocking Out" a Beaten Man.

Try and acquire the knack of keeping the time. By that piece of advice, I mean the noting of the seconds as they pass. For in all forms of contest, and in amateur ones particularly, it is wisest to save your serious attacks for the last half or three-quarters of a minute of each round. Try and save yourself by every means possible for the first two minutes or so, and then if you have worried and worked the other man sufficiently, you will have him at your mercy. He will be anxiously waiting for the call of time, while you are fresh and well. But in any event it is well to remember that judges and referees have a habit of paying more attention to what occurs during the last few seconds of a round than they do to its earlier incidents. The former are fresher in the memory for one thing, and thereby more likely to go down on their notes when apportioning the scores. Lead as often as you can then, for leads count.

No boxer whom I have ever seen could be compared with Tommy Burns in this very important quality. He seemed to keep an automatic clock in his head, by which he registered the flight of the seconds, and he was always ready to put in his most telling work at the end of every round. He might have appeared to be distressed and in bad trouble after the first half-minute, anxious to clinch, and apparently exhausted. You might have thought he was, be even sure of it; and yet somewhere about the 130th second he started in, as though he were only just beginning the fight. He was on wires and as full of vigour and energy as a young dog. He got to work with both hands, and positively seemed to

A Cross-Buttock Throw.

overwhelm his opponent with the fury of his attack. He might have been fighting for points instead of for a knock-out, as he usually was.

Which reminds me of one last piece of advice, and that is, to be always careful not to be fooled by any assumption of carelessness or weariness on the part of your adversary, even though it may appear that you have only to dash in to administer the coup de grâce. You may have the amplest grounds for assuming that his apparent weariness and exhaustion are genuine. You may indeed have him practically beaten to a standstill and incapable of further serious exertion, so that you may feel yourself fully justified in going in confidently to finish the business. It is, of course, desirable always to finish the bout definitely yourself, should opportunity arise, without leaving it to the verdict of the judges. To err is human, and they may not have credited you with as many points as you would yourself suppose them to have done. But in putting on your finishing touch you must always be cautious lest his apparently serious condition may not have been exaggerated until it constitutes a trap for the unwary. Go in and win by all means; never neglect the chance of " knocking-out " a dazed opponent, who may otherwise make .use of the time you have allowed him to recover his waning powers. Never give him a moment's peace until he is " out "; but go in with circumspection, feint before you hit, in case of accidents, and when you DO hit be sure that you hit hard and accurately.

Back Heeling after You Have Shaken with a Punch.

CHAPTER VII.

The Practical Value of Boxing as a Means of Defence against an Attack by Hooligans.

I WOULD unhesitatingly assert that for practical purposes the noble art of self-defence will be found far more valuable as a means of self-defence than either wrestling or even ju-jitsu, especially if the boxer himself has taken a few pains in acquiring a smattering of both these arts, neither of which by themselves would possess any particular advantage over even a good rough-and-tumble fighter.

In the disagreeable event of your running up against the hooligan, and such a misfortune may easily befall you, you have to decide on taking one of two courses, the first of which is to retreat as speedily as possible, and the second that of standing up and "facing the music." I take it that the latter will be the one which will commend itself as being the more congenial, to say nothing of being certainly the more dignified and possibly the safer, particularly if your assailant happens to prove fleeter of foot, besides which your evident determination to put him "through the mill" may remind him of an important engagement elsewhere.

We will suppose, however, that he is "all out" for blood, and that the question of superiority between you has to be decided right there, in which case you will do well to remember that you are very probably "up against a singularly stiff proposition,"

A Block to the Back Heel.

in which, though your study of the " Noble Art " will prove of no mean assistance, you will nevertheless be somewhat hampered by habits which have become almost second nature to you. In the first place, you will find it best to stand rather more edge on to him, as he attacks, than you would when engaged in a bout with the gloves. Should he come in with his arms whirling and intent to use his fists only, you can soon shift yourself into a comfortable posture, while if he comes kicking you will be well placed to guard with your left leg raised, with the foot turned well in, so as to take his kick well on the outside of your leg, where it won't hurt much, instead of on your shin, where it would be serious. If practised carefully, an excellent stop against a kicker is to stand rather square, and as he delivers his kick to raise your front leg so as to meet his shin on your heel. If the timing is accurate the kicker will collapse with a broken leg, but it must be accurate or you will come off badly.

If, however, you do not fancy taking a kick on your calf, and are not sure of your ability to meet it with your heel, you will find one portion of the tricky work of the schools useful, and that is, of course, a smart slip or side-step and pivot, which will leave him to rush madly past you, when, of course, you should let him have it good and hard in the jaw or neck.

By the way, if his rush gives you reason to retreat, it is best to go wide as well as back, and to do it in one movement, for the hooligan as a rule is a great believer in the virtues of " high-kicking," and that variety of " le savate " is unpleasant.

Countering a "Butter" with Knee Upper-cut.

Which reminds one that some slight knowledge of " le savate " is by no means valueless in such circumstances, but, as already mentioned, the boxer would in any event do well to acquire some knowledge of wrestling, either in one form or another. Such knowledge will in no way diminish his abilities for rapid movement, so essential to success in the ring, but will also prove of real practical value should he be called upon to put his fists to serious use in defence of his life, limbs, or property. And in the case of ruffianly assault it is his life which will be in danger. For he must be scrupulously careful to avoid being floored under any circumstances. When down he can have little hope of escaping serious attention from the feet of the " gentle " hooligan.

And there are several methods whereby one may lay oneself open to a fall in defending oneself against a street attack, especially when you and your adversary get to close quarters.

He may, for instance, get your head " in chancery." An unpleasant position in itself, but a highly dangerous one, if your enemy converts it into a " cross buttock," by stooping and swinging his hips round under you as he bends you over and then lifting you on to his shoulders to hurl you in a heap on to the ground. A most dangerous and deadly throw which he will almost certainly aggravate by falling on top of you.

In order to guard against this throw, don't waste time in pasting his chest and kidneys, as you would with an ordinary fair fighter, but supposing he has your head under his left arm, bring your right hand up from behind and seize him by his left shoulder, then, keeping your right leg behind his left, pull him back sharply over your knee or hip on to his back, hitting him in the face with your free hand as hard as you can as he goes. If your head should be under his right arm reverse proceedings.

Another useful throw which may be found profitable in this species of combat, should your antagonist have let go at your face and missed, his hand passing over your shoulder, is to grasp his extended arm with your opposite hand, and pushing the heel of your other hand hard up under his chin, forcing back his head, back-heeling him the while just below the knee, with your right or left leg against his corresponding one, according to circumstances; to throw all your weight forward, when he will come down pretty heavily.

Even if caught napping at this and only able to parry when pushed so far back as to be unable to throw your balance properly forward, you can avoid being thrown, and, by thrusting your fingers into his nostrils or eyes, compel him to draw back.

Should you be yourself so caught in this awkward hold your only method of escape is to step well back with your rear foot, so as to increase your stability, free your " clicked " leg as soon as possible, and meanwhile jab him in the face as hard as you can with your free hand. In any event you are in a very awkward position, and cannot hope to do yourself much good until you can free yourself, for with your chin forced back and all your energy concentrated on bracing yourself up with your rear leg, your short-arm jabs will not be very effective.

THE SIDNEY PRESS, BEDFORD.

A Selection Of Classic Instructive Titles Relating To
The Art Of Pugilism & Self Defence
In Both War & Peace
Find our entire selection @ naval-military-press.com

ALL-IN FIGHTING
The distilled knowledge of W.E. Fairbairn, legendary SOE instructor in unarmed combat, and inventor of the Sykes-Fairbairn knife, who learned his deadly skills in 30 years on the Shanghai waterfront.
Fully illustrated.
9781847348531

ART OF BOXING AND SCIENCE OF SELF DEFENCE
Former Lightweight Champion Billy Edwards shares the techniques and strategies of the sweet science in his beautifully illustrated boxing guide. Explore boxing's transition from bare knuckle spectacle to today's Marquis of Queensbury ruleset.
9781474539548

SELF DEFENCE OR THE ART OF BOXING
Ned Donnelly was a pioneer of boxing training during the late Victorian era. Explore the strategies and techniques used by this trainer of champions via a series of easy-to-follow illustrations and clear, concise coaching steps.
9781474539562

JACK GOODWIN'S BOXING
This 1920's boxing masterpiece by Jack Goodwin puts you in the shoes of a coach in that era. Uncover the best ways to run, manage and train boxers as taught by Jack Goodwin, a champion and trainer of champions in the noble science.
9781474539586

ART OF WRESTLING
George de Relwyskow Army Gymnastic Staff
In the appreciation to this book Captain Daniels, V.C., M.C., Rifle Brigade, states: "In adding a word to this book on the style of wrestling as taught at the Headquarters Gymnasium of the British Army, and having had personal experience in the various holds and throws taught, I consider it has been of great value in the training of the soldier, and the bringing out of those qualities of grit and determination which have been seen in all ranks who have taken an active part throughout the greatest war in history." 1919.
9781783313563

BOXING (V-Five)
The Aviation Training Office of the Chief of Naval Operations
The game-changing V-Five suite of training manuals helped get a generation of American aviators fit for war. Here we explore how the airmen of the US navy trained in boxing as part of their military fitness regime.
9781474539623

WRESTLING (V-Five)
The Aviation Training Office of the Chief of Naval Operations
The game-changing V-Five suite of training manuals helped get a generation of American aviators fit for war. Here we explore how the airmen of the US navy trained in collegiate wrestling as part of their military fitness regime.
9781474539685

THE TEXTBOOK OF WRESTLING
Get your wrestling skills matt-ready from wrestling champion and world-renown trainer Ernest Gruhn. Replete with detailed holds, throws, pins and strategies for success in a wide range of wrestling rulesets.
9781474539647

KILL OR GET KILLED
Rex Applegate's "kill or be killed" helped prepare America's marines, soldiers, sailors, spies and airmen for the realities of war. This highly shared and respected work provides all you need to know about unarmed combat and close quarter engagement with the enemy.
9781474539661

MANUAL OF PHYSICAL TRAINING 1914
(United States Army)
Published just prior to the outbreak of World War 1, this beautifully illustrated guide was designed to revolutionise the combat fitness and readiness of the US Army covering a wide range of gymnastic and combat calisthenic exercises.

DEAL THE FIRST DEADLY BLOW
United States Department of the Army

This Vietnam-era classic showcases in detail how the US Forces trained in close quarter combat. Known as the "encyclopaedia of combat" it helped a generation learn how to become devastating effective with empty hands, knives and bayonets alike.

9781474539722

HAND-TO-HAND COMBAT
Bureau of Aeronautics U.S Navy 1943

This is one of the best combative manuals from World War 2, developed by the US Navy V-Five Staff, that included the renowned American wrestler Wesley Brown. It is then not especially surprising that wrestling skills predominate in this manual, and form the base skill-set for this combative system.

9781474537391

ABWEHR ENGLISCHER GANGSTER METHODEN DEFENSE OF ENGLISH GANGSTERS METHODS – SILENT KILLING – FULL ENGLISH TRANSLATION

In 1942 the Wehrmacht published a training manual with the goal of countering the "silent killing" tactics used by the British commando units. The manual was – much in line with typical National Socialist terminology –titled

"Abwehr Englischer Gangster-methoden" or "Defence Against English Gangster methods".

This book was compiled due the Wehrmacht intelligence operatives uncovering of a British hand-to-hand course for the SOE, Commandos, et al, on methods of quick and silent killing (undoubtedly developed by W. E. Fairbairn and E. A. Sykes). They correctly assessed that their troops in general and particularly the Geheime Staatspolizei (Gestapo), Sicherheitsdienst (SD), their security guards, and sentries would be in grave danger when confronted by men trained in these methods. This manual/program was the Wehrmacht's response.

9781474538336

HAND TO HAND COMBAT

Francois d'Eliscu taught thousands of U.S. Army Rangers how to fight down and dirty in World War II. d'Eliscu doesn't get the press that Fairbairn and Applegate do, but he did a commendable job writing this book. It is basic, meant for training raw recruits in a short amount of time before sending them to the front, but simple is good when you are in combat, as most combative experts' will tell you.

9781474535823

WE Fairbairn's Complete Compendium of Lethal, Unarmed, Hand-to-Hand Combat Methods and Fighting In Colour

All 844 images of Fairbairn and his assistants can now for the first time be seen in full colour, lending a clarity to the practical methods of mastering the manner of dealing with an assailant, both in time of war and when placed in difficulty during unpleasant modern urban situations. These various holds, trips, kicks, blows etc, allow the average man or woman a position of security against almost any form of armed or unarmed attack.

Captain W.E. Fairbairn would have approved of this new colour version, that gives an illustrative clarity to the original that was lacking in previous monochrome reprints of his work.

All six of W.E. Fairbairn's works in one binding to create the ultimate colour compendium: Get Tough-All-In Fighting-Shooting to Live-Scientific Self-Defence-Hands Off!-Defendu

9781783318735

BOXING FOR BOYS

Regtl. Sergt.-Major & B Dent Army Gymnastic Headquarters

A successful system of boxing instruction for large classes, to allow tuition with no detriment to the "backward or shy pupil". Covers Kit-On, Guard-Sparring-Advance-Point & Mark-Ducking-Medicine, Bag-Left & Right Hooks etc. The author considered that boxing systematically taught to the youth was beneficial exercise, and would have a marked elevating influence on the national character.

9781783314607

HAND-TO-HAND FIGHTING

A System Of Personal Defence For The Soldier (1918)

A tough book on the art of hand to hand fighting in the trenches of the Great War. Demonstrating techniques utilised to "do away with the enemy", many of which are barred in clean wrestling, the book includes good clear photographic illustrations presenting important attack methods including the "Hammer Lock", "Kidney Kick", "Head Twist", "Knee Groin Kick", and the "Knee Break", all very important in a man to man, life or death encounter, when fighting in the mud of the trenches.

9781783313983

www.ingramcontent.com/pod-product-compliance
Lightning Source LLC
Chambersburg PA
CBHW070326100426
42743CB00011B/2582